The Dark Side of a K-POP Idol

-The Untold Truth-

Written by S.C. Leon

Table of Contents

COPYRIGHT PROTECTION 3
INTRODUCTION 1
CHAPTER ONE: WHAT IS KPOP 4
21st century: Beginning of the Hallyu Wave 6
How Is K-Pop Different from western music? 6
CHAPTER TWO: BTS AND BLACKPINK 14
K-pop or gay-pop 16
Boys challenge norms, girls reinforce them 17
Being real is the new deal 19
CHAPTER THREE: THE BIG NAMES IN KPOP 21
The Pioneers of K-Pop 21
Who spread K-Pop in Asia? 24
Who brought K-Pop to the world? 26
CHAPTER FOUR: IDOL GROUPS & THEIT STRUCTURE 27
Famous K-Pop Group Leaders 27
Famous K-Pop Vocalists 29
Famous K-Pop Rappers 30
Famous K-Pop Dancers 30
Famous K-Pop Sub-Units 31
Famous K-Pop Visuals 32
Famous K-Pop Maknae 32

Famous K-Pop 4Ds 33
Differences in K-pop girls and K-pop boy groups 34
Why do they split and go solo? 36
CHAPTER FIVE: K-POP CHARACTERISTICS 38
Hybrid genre and transnational values 38
Criticism of hybrid identity 43
Marketing 44
Choreography 45
Fashion 47
Government support 51
Copyrights 53
CHAPTER SIX: THE DARK SIDES OF THE KPOP INDUSTRY ..54
Music Executives Have Extreme Control over Stars' Personal Lives 55
Many Idols Go Through a 10-Year Pop Star Boot Camp 55
Idols Are Expected To Get Plastic Surgery 56
Managers Reportedly Blackmail Their Idols 57
Music Agencies Allegedly Pimp Their Trainees to Sponsors 58
Idols Resort to Starvation to Achieve the 'Perfect' Body Image 59
Some Idols Follow the Extreme 'Paper Cup Diet' 59
Fans Go To Extreme Lengths to Get Close With Stars 60
Managers and Executives Take Advantage of Rising Stars 61
Idols Regularly Faint Onstage 62
Idols Often Take Years to Make Money 62
Anti-Fans Sometimes Try To Kill Idols 64
Racism & Cultural Insensitivity Abound In The Idol Industry 64

Being LGBTQ+ Is Considered Taboo, Although a Few Stars Have Come Out 65

A Misogynistic Double Standard Exists When It Comes To Male & Female Idols 66

Idols Aren't Allowed to Date Other Stars 67

Music Agencies Foster Intense Rivalries between Girl Groups 68

Struggling With Mental Health Is Stigmatized 68

Slave Contracts Are Normal 69

The hours are nuts 71

CHAPTER SEVEN: THE DIFFICULT LIFE OF A KPOP IDOL 73

Why Life In The Business Is Hard 73

Copyright © 2019

COPYRIGHT PROTECTION

All rights reserved. No part of this publication may be reproduced, distributed, or transmitted in any form or by any means, including photocopying, recording, or other electronic or mechanical methods, without the prior written permission of the publisher, except in the case of brief quotations embodied in critical reviews and certain other noncommercial uses permitted by copyright law.

This book is 100% independent and unofficial and is not endorsed by and has no connection with the people it features nor with any organization or individual connection what so ever with the people of persons featured. Every care has been taken into researching this book, but due to the nature of the subject matter, some information may change over time. With CC attribution and fair use of imagery and information for the purpose of education and information, in no way is this publication aimed to hurt any individual.

INTRODUCTION

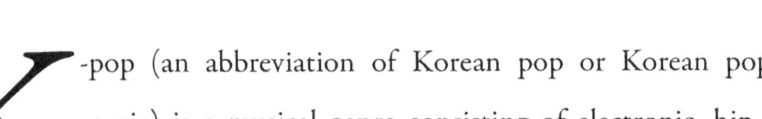

K-pop (an abbreviation of Korean pop or Korean popular music) is a musical genre consisting of electronic, hip hop, pop, rock, and R&B music originating in South Korea. Korean pop is a musical genre that originates in South Korea, and it is characterized by varieties of audio-visual elements.

In addition to music, K-pop has grown into a popular subculture among teenagers & young adults throughout Asia, resulting in widespread interest in the fashion & style of Korean idol groups & singers.

The formation of Seo Taiji & boys ushered in kpop in 1992. The group was known for its experimentation in different music styles, and that brought about a significant shift in the entertainment sector of South Korea.

Back in 2012, the Gangnam Style of Psy made the whole world aware of Korean pop. Then the world saw kpop as a subset of the Korean pop music section, which was centered on girls and boys idol groups. It's worthy of mentioning that kpop has in fact been flourishing long before the introduction of Gangnam style and it has been drawing crowds from

South East Asia and Japan as far as the early 2000s. In recent times that is in the late 2000s, kpop is rooted in the other parts of Asia and the rest of the world, which includes the Middle East region that no one thought kpop would reach.

Kpop isn't the first shot of Korea at music in the global entertainment sector. As far as the 1950s, Korean movies have attracted accolades from all over the place, with one of the awards being the 2012 Golden Lion awarded to Pieta. There is also the Winter Sonata that became a major hit in Japan, which gave way for success stories in East Asia. Now, successes were recorded in the past. All share one thing in common; they are either restricted to a particular area or limited in quantity. But it is different with kpop, kpop differs in many ways from past successes. For one, kpop has been around for about 15 years, which is a tad longer than the reigning years of Hong Kong movies or the Japanese "J-pop" wave that was common in the 1990s.

It's also worthy to note that kpop groups have been a consistent hit on charts around the world enough for the billboard to create a "K-pop Hot 100" world chart in 2012 and YouTube to include a kpop entry in its musical listings. In recent times, kpop isn't restricted to a particular region or specific age groups. No! Kpop is now attracting large audiences all over the world. Today, not only teens and twenties kpop but adults and parents inclusive. As a matter of fact, kpop isn't only for the native populations but also immigrants native to US and Europe.

K-pop has now even spread across the world, thanks to the internet. People all over the world now enjoy K-pop, even though they don't necessarily understand the words. K-pop has formed many lifelong friendships, & I hope this will be the case for you too! Join me in the next chapter to discuss in details what K-Pop really is, the history & their differences from western music, the characteristics of kpop groups, the bad sides of kpop as well as the factors that makes life in the business hard for kpop idols.

CHAPTER ONE: WHAT IS KPOP

K-Pop or K-Pop is short for "Korean Pop". It can refer to the whole of popular music in Korea, but is often used in a narrower sense to describe the genre that has dominated the Korean music market for about the last 20 years. This genre incorporates elements of western pop, dance, electronic, R&B and Hip Hop - but after years of experience music makers & producers in South Korea know how to "home-make" successful hits with a distinctive sound different from its formerly western roots.

Like many South-Asian countries the area of today's South Korea underwent a series of foreign influences that led to the development of its very own popular music market. During Japanese occupation (1910-1945) local and foreign composers created a mix of traditional Korean music and Gospel that is popular until today and known as "Trot".

The end of Japan's brutal colonial rule marked the arrival of Westernization - taking place in a lot of areas of South Korean life, also leading to a change in the sound of the Trot genre. Western music began to be aired on radio and Western-style clubs popped up in various locations to cater to the American soldiers still stationed in South Korea. Not only did many Korean musicians let themselves be influenced by the jazz, blues, country and rock & roll sound of the West, but the Korean public, too, took an interest in them.

South Korea's own music industry started blooming in the 60s alongside the economy, and produced it's very first own big names, labels and talent contests. The 70s marked a time of Hippie folk pop, as well as the arrival of DJ culture, followed by the 80s as the "era of ballads".

What we know today as "K-Pop" first emerged more distinctively in the 1990s. Newer music groups produced up-beat, catchy songs with lyrics that dealt with the everyday problems of Korean society, paving the way for the modern sound of K-Pop. The mid- and late 90s saw the founding of major music labels that dominate the market today and underground music movements of hip hop and rock first managing to gain main stream success.

21st century: Beginning of the Hallyu Wave

The beginning of the 21st century marked the beginning of the global Korean wave. Not everyone knows it's going on, but taken from the fact you are reading this article to an extent you have seen changes around you (or at least online). Korean industry managers & music producers did not sit down together and started to plot world dominance (or have they?), but the last 15 years have seen an increased global interest in Korean culture, especially entertainment goods such as Korean TV dramas and Korean Pop music.

Today South Korea has a lively Indie Rock, Hip Hop & Dance-Pop scene. But other countries have colorful music scenes, too. Then what's so special about K-Pop that has risen to international fame? You will read more about this!

How Is K-Pop Different from western music?

So you have a rough idea what K-Pop is. Maybe you have heard some already - now you are wondering - what makes K-Pop different from

Western pop-music? This is supposed to be enrichment to my life? How exactly?

Returning quickly to our definition of K-Pop before - the music we are about to discuss is the popular music in South Korea that is mainly produced for commercial reasons. As mentioned in Step 1, South Korea also has a thriving Indie scene - but what we want to talk about here is the music, generally known as "*K-Pop*".

Enough with the theory, let's have a 1st taste of what K-Pop is (probably you have seen or heard K-Pop before, but anyway) - let's watch a music video together:

What you have just seen is a music video by one of the most successful K-Pop girl groups of our time, "Girls' Generation". For some more comparison, here is a music video by a K-Pop boy group:

What you watched just now is a music video by K-Pop boy group "B.A.P" (an acronym for "Best Absolute Perfect" - daring, huh?), a group who debuted in 2012 and is already on world tour. Or perhaps BTS, being the Bulletproof Boy Scouts.

Maybe you have had a few WTF-moments while watching these two videos. Let me assure you - before we lose you here - there are many types of K-Pop videos. If this is not your style, there's a lot more BAP

Hurricane1that is quite different. Speaking from experience - I would have not liked these videos myself if you showed them to me (about 2, 5 years ago), but now I love them. So keep a open mind.

When you first get into K-Pop, it's not so important to know who is who, but - do I like it? That's a question that we will turn to in the due course of this 10 Step Guide, but 1st let's do a quick comparison of some general rules that K-Pop songs and videos abide to - in contrast to those of the Western pop industry.

1. The people who are the faces for the music (which is of course, just like Western Pop, produced by a whole company of people - stylists, sound engineers, camera men, managers, etc.)

are generally young, above-averagely attractive and can Girls Generation The Boys1 either sing, rap, dance or have a minimum amount of charisma. The same goes for K-Pop groups: Young individuals who decide they want to enter the music business, often giving up school or college for their dreams.

2. Maybe you belong to the group of people who have a problem with the modern idea of "star" (join the club): A person so high above all "normal individuals" they are truly "god-like" and "untouchable". Of course lots of K-Pop idols are marketed the very same way. They are used as trend-setters, so that people will buy their EPs, merchandise & style their hair after the ever-changing trends. Who these young singers and dancers really are often gets lost and they play a role for the camera.

3. When it comes to the music - it's less for artistic purpose or emotional release of the song writer - it's meant to sell. But just like in most cultures, the music reflects the hopes, dreams and problems of the younger generation of its one people. The topics are of course romantic feelings, dreams, the search for meaning in life and the sadness over what's wrong in one's own life or the world. And yes, partying.

4. The melody beat & vocals are all mixed to be ultimately catchy and like western pop-music - less avant-garde and more appealing to the mainstream. Most songs have sing-a-long-ability and rather than being an in-depth musical experience, they are commonly light-hearted and fun. A lot of pop music (no matter where it comes from) has been looked down upon by fans of other music genres and is nothing more than "guilty-pleasure" music for those listening to a range of music styles.

5. Most likely you have seen pop artist's debut and your thoughts were basically: "Ahem, ok, Pop music is averagely pretty low standard, but this is so low that I don't even know where to place it on the scale…" Without naming names, people with very little talent get produced in most countries (or the other way around - the person actually is talented, but their producer sucks and auto-tunes them anyway), and what's even sadder - some of them the boys SDSN become successful, teenage-heart-breaking mega stars. I'm not going to claim that this doesn't happen in K-Pop, but K-Pop averagely has a higher standard of quality.

6. As the concept of "boy groups" and "girl groups" is all well and thriving in South Korea, solo artists present a minority in the face of pop groups with member sizes from 4 - 12. These

young (wannabe-) stars start training, after having been accepted at a talent agency, in very harsh and intensive programs to perfect their dancing and singing skills and to generally prepare for the stressful and demanding life of a national star.

This raises the bar, as although the industry is dominated by few big agencies, there is constant competition between already famous groups trying to stay at the top of the charts, before the younger rookies catch up and take over.

7. Most importantly of all: K-Pop was till rather recently (the last 2-3 years) majorly produced by Koreans for Koreans. Though some groups and solo singers produce English versions of their songs today, most of K-Pop is in Korean, sprinkled with bits of (not always correct) English. This is something to get used to - unless you know Korean, you will not understand 90% of the lyrics. Being a lyric-maniac myself, I found this bothersome for some time. But I have come to not only enjoy the sound of the foreign language that is Korean (to me) - I also appreciate the fact, that 6some songs as sweet/nice/cool as they sound, in fact have some really lame/stupid/cliché lyrics, which I can happily ignore and just appreciate for their sound - as I do not understand them.

8. Now to the content of K-Pop music videos, which are important parts of the experience? Although themes, costumes and lights change - there are certain patterns: 4A large portion of the video is spent showing the members dancing, another large part showing close-ups of the members faces or them interacting while singing/rapping and then some videos attempt to tell a story with a (not always coherent) plot.

   As mentioned: Competition in the K-Pop industry is tough, this means that a lot of effort is put into producing music videos, which are aiming to be ultimately always newer, more interesting and more extravagant than before. And while- yes - we see approaches (like the two music videos above) very similar to Western pop music videos, you'll also get to see some stuff you are not so likely to see on this scale in other country's music scenes.

9. As you may have noticed - partially the K-Pop boys & girls look westernized, but then again - they don't. Guys wearing eye liner? Yes. Eye liner... Plenty of it... In recent years South Korea has seen a trend which is known in the West as something called "Flower Boys". Boys/Young men (& girls) don't actually street-wear all the crazy outfits of K-Pop idols,

but an 11certain androgynous look has taken over most of K-Pop male idols.

This look is often described with the wise words "gayyyyy" by a number of Westerners, but it is simply a fashion trend, which can actually highlight and enhance the facial features of male individuals, as much as females.

10. Part of listening and watching K-Pop is to keep an open mind. Yes, it's also a selling of close-to-impossible ideals about looks, coolness, sexiness and charisma, but it's the approach of a culture so different from your own (yes, even if you are Chinese or Japanese or especially then - you will know the Korean way of things is different (and highly diverse in itself)) you are guaranteed to be surprised, emotionally slapped in the face a couple of times and to learn how to be a lot more open minded about a lot of things.

CHAPTER TWO: BTS AND BLACKPINK

As an inhabitant of planet with access to an internet TV will have noted, boy band BTS and girl group Blackpink are seismically moving & shaking the global music scene, surfing a tidal wave of K-pop as it crashes upon global shores.

The exposure of the two super-groups recently sky-rocketed to ever greater heights when, one after the other, they smashed YouTube records of Most Viewed Clips in the first 24 hours. Blackpink was first with Kill This Love ringing up 56.7 million views. Barely 24 hours later, had BTS shattered that number, raising it by 20 million views, with Boys with Luv.

So has K-pop as a genre truly gone global? Or is it simply that, as the world goes gaga over the Bantang Boys, BTS is dragging Blackpink in its foaming wake? The two groups come from the same place and are often mentioned in the same breath. But when it comes to sales, the chasm between them is glaring.

In 2019, Blackpink's EP Kill This Love broke the record for the highest first-day sales for a girl group album with 78 275 copies sold, according to Hanteo. Compare that to BTS: The Bantang Boys pre-sold 2.6 million copies of their latest album Map of the Soul: Persona, according to Billboard.

BTS is also a phenomenon in a way that Blackpink just are not. BTS paid homage to pop gods The Beatles who they've been compared to repeatedly in terms of their effect on fans, and in the transformative power of pop culture when they appeared on The Late Show with Stephen Colbert. Their performance there deliberately mirrored the Fab Four's world-shaking appearance on The Ed Sullivan Show in 1964.

While Blackpink might be garnering YouTube views by the million and filling concert hall seats by the tens of thousands, they cannot compare with the thunderous buzz that surrounds BTS who are, arguably the biggest band in the world today and the biggest Asian act of modern times.

Of course, this is nothing new in the music world. Some acts were always more popular than others and this has never stopped a genre from having massive success. But there is a boy band-girl group undertone to the BTS-Blackpink dynamic, and on the gender-expectation front, Blackpink has limited room for maneuver. That is not the case with BTS and other Korean boy bands, who are turning Asian and global norms of "masculinity" on their heads.

K-pop or gay-pop

How do we blur gender norms? Asked Michael Hurt, a professor of Cultural Studies at the Hankuk University of Foreign Studies in Seoul, one way to do that is dressing up women as tomboys but that's nothing new. On the contrary, Korea is creating another definition of sexiness for men.

In today's social media era, when gender neutrality and fluidity is very much to the fore, Korean boy bands are redefining maleness with the "flower boy" concept of the pretty, pure, gentleman. K-pop men do things that have traditionally been associated with, well, women: They wear make-up, dress up, act cute and show that they care.

Among some Western males, this form of masculinity is derided as being "gay." Millions of Western girls and women, however, have clearly been smitten. And as online pundit ask a Korean has often noted: Korean boy groups have tens of thousands of women screaming their names during concerts. If that's not masculinity - what is?

Hurt calls the "flower boy" trend a new form of "hyper-masculinity" and compares it to a fashion show: Models hit catwalks sporting styles that are not designed for everyday wear but will spark and define trends and conversations in the real world. This is new. Meanwhile, girl groups like Blackpink are stuck with a sexualized presentation format that dates back to pre-history.

Boys challenge norms, girls reinforce them

Pretty dancing girls is an old formula and Korea does it well. They maxed out the way you can harness the female body for economic gain. Maxed out, indeed, however, the problem for Korean girl groups does not stop at being unable to upgrade an already highly sexualized image. At home, girl bands are subject to societal pressures that their male counterparts have been able to challenge.

Blackpink is just a harder sell than BTS," John Lie of UC Berkeley's Sociology Department told Asia Times. Boy groups project an image that they're well-built physically and they're nice, romantic guys. It's the contrary of what South Korean society actually is, which is, at the core, very masculinist and misogynistic.

So, while the boy bands are bringing something new to the table the "flower boy" look and concept girl groups are stuck. While boy groups reflect a difference with Korean culture itself, girl groups are closer to what Korean society projects. In K-pop, women are submissive, cute and sexy: their self-presentation is not that much at odds with how South Korean women are expected to act. Still, even flower boys can be very, very bad boys.

Lie noted that the ongoing Burning Sun scandal in which multiple A-list K-pop male celebrities have been named and shamed in a sex trafficking, drugs and bribery ring centered on the Burning Sun night club in Seoul's funky Gangnam district - exposes the hypocrisy of at least some male bands' idealistic images.

The scandal, though, probably won't affect K-pop as a whole: After all, the genre's top names, BTS and Blackpink, are not implicated. The question now is what will drive the genre forward.

Being real is the new deal

According to Bernie Cho, a Seoul-based industry player with DFSB Kollective, the future of K-pop is not about gender, it is about how truly global the genre can go. In that sense, both BTS and Blackpink point to a new future including Monsta X from 2015 has grown fast.

BTS can sing, rap, or chat comfortably in Korean, English or Japanese, Blackpink goes even further as they have members who can also communicate in Chinese and Thai. Moreover, unlike most Asian music, K-Pop artist names and song titles are often provided in a bilingual Korean-English format, Cho noted.

For the music industry executive, BTS, Monsta X and Blackpink represent a new kind of act in K-pop where being highly trained singers or dancers is not enough.

BTS are actual authentic artists who play key roles in producing, composing and writing lyrics to their own hits, even Blackpink can't be placed in the 'just cute' category. If they ever wanted to be a live band, they could pull it off.

Rather than being carefully curated products manufactured on factory-line production process the previous formula for K-pop acts - BTS and Blackpink indicate that it is now about being artists, rather than simply performers. The 'fake it 'till you makes it' days are over. Being real is the deal now...authenticity has displaced automation as the new normal.

CHAPTER THREE:
THE BIG NAMES IN KPOP

Have you had enough of all the theory in this eBook and want somewhere to actually get started? Here it comes: The Big Names of K-Pop. Who makes this crazy (not-so) little thing called K-Pop?

You know some about the history of K-Pop already and how there were different eras, where different genres and sub-genres of music dominated the industry. It's time not to ask "which music genre?", but "who introduced this stuff in the 1st place"? If you recall, you'll remember that - yes - a number of legendary western artists influenced the Korean music industry (in the long-gone and more recent past), but the music style that has emerged within the last 10 years has finally managed to really create a unique sound, that though similar to some Western music goes its own paths and directions and is influenced by different trends.

The Pioneers of K-Pop

We have mentioned the shift from the "era of ballads" to the up-beat colorful dance-pop that K-Pop majorly is today. What triggered this shift can be traced back to one significant event: The debut of (then rookie) group Seo Taiji & Boys on the talent show of MBC.

They are the group credited with bringing a new sound to the Korean music scene and becoming instantly successful, despite their low score on the talent show. (Fun Fact: Did you know that Papa YG was a member of Seo Taiji & Boys? Also – Seo Taiji, although in his 40s and not having released any music since 2009, is one of the highest paid celebrities, receiving $2,000,000,000 Won (roughly $200,000) for an appearance on TV). Anyway, their new sound was not only much catchier and some fresh wind in the South Korean music scene, it also came with lyrics that actually reflected everyday problems of the general public. Other musicians soon followed in their footsteps and the 1st K-Hip-Hop groups and artists were born.

In 1995 SM Entertainment was founded, most of the groups and singers in the South Korean music market "were born" through an entertainment agency, which gives auditions and picks out youngsters to train for a (potential) life of fame. SM is one of the 1st such agencies founded and remains until today one of the most influential K-Pop-producing agencies.

In the late 1990s YG Entertainment, JYP Entertainment and DSP Media followed. As the artists they produced bloomed and blossomed (at least sales-wise) these agencies gained so much influence in the music scene, that rather than the groups themselves giving fame to the agencies - it was the other way around! A rookie group would gain attention through the fact that they were produced by a big name company (which remains a major factor in the K-Pop industry till today).

What allowed the industry to grow over such a short time to such an extent? Well, 1st of all - popular music now sounded differently and more accessible to a whole new audience: Teenagers. Agencies - smart as they were - soon realized the potential of targeting a younger crowd of listeners and just how to do so successfully: Idol groups - young male and female singers, not much older than their audience, doing cool dances and singing catchy songs. The 1st group that emerged and is today considered an "idol group" was H.O.T.

Seo Taiji & Boys and H.O.T (and fellow 90s musicians) are listed among the inspirations to enter the music business of many idols we know today. Other successful groups included Shinhwa (a male group still active today) and the girl groups (DSP's) Fin.K.L and (SM's) S.E.S (Fun Fact: K-Pop group names always were quite strange... and I mean really strange. One popular boy group of the 90s was called "Sechs Kies" – which is supposed to be German for "six crystals" – it actually means "six gravel"... gravel being singular (source for this: I'm a native speaker of German). Fun Fact 2: Did you know Lee Hyori was a member of Fin.K.L?)

And the 2nd reason for the rise of who became known as "the big 3": The popularity of K-Pop started spreading to other countries. "The Big 3" – SM, YG and JYP Entertainment's artists caught the attentions of non-Korean audiences at the start of 21st century...

Who spread K-Pop in Asia?

For a long time in Modern History (the last 100 years) it was expected/feared, that Japanese popular culture would not only highly influence the Korean one, but even take it over. Manga, Anime and to an extend J-Pop & J-Rock have gained some international popularity, but in fact today it's not the Koreans listening to and importing Japanese music, but the other way around. How and why is that?

For a long time after the Japanese occupation South Korea had very strong restrictions put on any imported goods from Japan to prevent cultural influence. Those were lifted in 1998 (possibly as consequence of the 1997 Asian financial crisis) and a new strategy was put into action by the South Korean government to prevent a Japanese cultural invasion. Namely – the Ministry for Culture requested a large increase of budget to invest into the home entertainment industry, to set up departments and create the system of auditioning and training of potential pop stars, as it exists until today.

Korean TV Dramas and music videos started to air in China and H.O.T and girl group Baby V.O.X were soon selling out concerts and masses of records in neighbor countries China and Japan, as well as Thailand. Other K-Pop artists who helped K-Pop invade fellow Asian countries and teenage minds were solo artists Bi Rain and BoA, alongside YG's Big Bang and SM's TVXQ joining the scene 2003-2006 (all these artists also released songs in Japanese!). Although TVXQ debuted prior to Big Bang, it was the latter group who really shaped to sound of K-Pop as we know it today by introducing electronica into the musical soup that K-Pop was and is – taking influences from Hip Hop, R&B, Electronic, Dance and Jazz.

Who brought K-Pop to the world?

In the hopes of attracting truly world-wide audiences a number of Korean groups and solo artists have tried and released English songs and albums. However none of this caused any actual breakthroughs – what did gain K-Pop a truly international audience was the emergence of internet platforms such as YouTube. This helped a number of K-Pop videos to go viral and supported the careers of following groups and artists. . It started with Super Junior followed by Girls Genereation, after many groups BTS BlackPink and Monsta X is ruling the world of K-pop.

CHAPTER FOUR:
IDOL GROUPS & THEIT STRUCTURE

If you have some experience with K-Pop seen some music videos, researched some stuff you might have noticed that different members have different tasks inside their respective group. But what tasks, positions are there? What do they really mean?

Let's start with the number of members: The average K-Pop group has between 4 to 6 members. As you might have noticed, most K-Pop groups have members who are all of the same gender. Groups of mixed gender are very rare so are solo artists. But to that again another time! Now these 4-6 members who does what? And what happens when there are 9 or 13 members?

Famous K-Pop Group Leaders

In most K-Pop groups there is a group leader, most of the time the leader will be the oldest member of the group or at least one of the older members. In other cases not the oldest member was chosen, but a member who was in-between the various ages in the group and thus able to connect both to the older and younger members.

A leader is expected to be mature and charismatic and be able to handle the attention and focus that is often on them. Their most important task is to take care of the other members, to motivate the group and to represent them in various ways. Many groups actually live together in dorms after debuting and need to get along thus needing a mediator and someone ensuring group harmony.

In a few cases there are leader-less groups. Some have adopted a concept to keep all members "equal" by not officially appointing a leader (e.g. JYP's Miss A). In other cases the former leader has left the group (JYP's 2PM) or in the rather unique case of JYJ, all members separated from their earlier group, leaving the leader behind and not officially chose a new leader.

Famous K-Pop Vocalists

Yes, it does help if you can actually sing when you are a k-pop idol. Members with the strongest vocal abilities get picked to be a Vocalist. Many groups have several vocalists, so there is often an official hierarchy of who gets to sing 1st and how much of a song:

1. The Main Vocalist - member who often (but not always) gets a lot of lines to sing in a song, sings the vocally challenging parts, has the strongest vocal ability, likely to receive solo parts
2. The Lead Vocalist - during verses usually sings before the Main Vocalist ("leads" into the song), often sings the chorus, substitute for the Main Vocalist in case of sickness/injury/etc.
3. The Sub Vocalist - supports Main and Lead Vocalist, gets only few lines of the song

In a group with numerous members there are often several Sub Vocalists and/or Lead Vocalists and even several Main Vocalists. In other groups song parts might be differently distributed, less planned and there might be no clear distinction between Vocalists.

Famous K-Pop Rappers

Rappers and Rapping is an essential part of most K-Pop group's music. Some might focus on rap and have more of an Hip-Hop orientated style (e.g. YG's Big Bang or Block B), while other groups will have more singing than rapping (e.g. Starship's Sistar or Woollim's Infinite). Just like with the vocalists, there is a hierarchy, if a group has more than one rapper.

1. The Main Rapper - gets most of the rapping parts, supposed to be the one with the best technique and rapping skills
2. The Lead Rapper - usually begins rapping parts, skills supposed to be good, too, but 2nd to the Main Rapper

Some groups don't have rappers, but its common practice to have at least 1 included in the group.

Famous K-Pop Dancers

You have probably seen a K-Pop music video before in which almost always you can see the group dancing and most of the time all of them dance. So aren't they all dancers? Yes, sure, but some will during performances and in music videos be more in the background, while others will get more difficult parts and even solo dances. Again, the familiar hierarchy:

1. The Main Dancer - expected to have great dancing skills, focuses less on singing / has fewer parts during songs / might even have only sub-vocal-parts (as breath needs to be saved for spectacular dances), will get solo dance parts
2. The Lead Dancer - as the whole group dances, the Lead Dancer will lead the group and dance in front, when all are dancing together

Some groups don't emphasize dancing so much, so they might not have the positions of Main and Lead Dancer assigned to members.

Famous K-Pop Sub-Units

A group that enjoys a lot of success might create a sub-unit. The sub-unit will consist of a smaller number of members (between 2 to 4 people usually) and is often used for more experimental releases or for trying an alternative music style, with members of an otherwise genre-mono-gamic group. Sometimes a sub-unit is created to release music in a different language (e.g. Mandarin or Japanese).

The members chosen for the sub-unit are most likely to be the more popular members of a group, but might also be the two oldest/youngest or people with whose name a funny sub-unit name can be formed. Such a sub-unit might also be made up of members of two different groups (which are under same music label) - e.g. the special unit

"Trouble Maker" made up of B2ST's JS and 4Minute's Hyuna. Some bigger groups even have several sub-units (e.g. SM's Super Junior has 5 sub-units in total)!

Famous K-Pop Visuals

Yes, K-Pop emphasizes and sells beauty. There is even a position in most K-Pop groups, that whoever has it must especially take care of their looks because that's one important thing they add to the group: Eye-candy. This position is not fan-made it's an actual thing. When a group introduces themselves on stage or on TV, one member might say "Hello. My name is ----------. I'm the Visual." The Visual is simply put the member who is considered most attractive and is likely to be the one most often hired to endorse products and appear in commercials and ads. Again, the choice of the visual might irritate newbies to K-Pop (and not-so-newbies, too), as Korean beauty standards are somewhat... east of Western ones.

Famous K-Pop Maknae

In K-pop, the term 'maknae' is the proportionate term of being the youngest member, which is famously known in the K-Pop world. In numerous boy groups, maknaes are valuable for the hyungs in light of the fact that they are like the baby of the family. They are normally observed as the cutest and the most childish of the group and the one that gets the most love from the hyungs. In any case, once in a while, the maknaes are not only playful but are also caring, matured, understanding, and adorable also. These talented, attractive, and cute maknaes are the pride of each group.

Famous K-Pop 4Ds

The 4D is not an official group position. It's a title of honor fans assign to the ... weirdest member of group. The person who says the most random and puzzling things on TV and who posts funny pictures of themselves on Twitter and generally enjoys being different. Like a .... Very special little snowflake yeah... To clarify: The title "4D" is not an insult - fans assign it to a group member, because their peculiarity is appealing or adorable. In some cases a member has even been called "8D", when they seem almost extraterrestrial.

Now you know the many different positions inside a K-Pop group. Remember: One member can have and usually has more than one task/position. For example: 4Minute's Hyuna is the Main Rapper, Main Dancer, Sub Vocalist and Visual of her group.

So... what about K-Pop group members playing instruments? Writing songs? Any of that happening, actually yes, but it's not the norm. A number of groups do stand out with members (co-)writing lyrics, music and playing instruments but for most groups the members are limited to the positions above.

Differences in K-pop girls and K-pop boy groups

There are a bunch of people claiming "K-pop boy groups have better concepts" or " K-pop girl groups have better concepts" but rarely ever "both boy groups and girl groups have amazing and diverse concepts"

There are differences in K-pop girls and K-pop boy groups, For K-pop girls group, all cute, all about innocent young love, soft pastel aesthetic, cute voices along with cute dances. For Kpop boy group, all rough and somewhat vulgar with lyrics and choreography, must show abs and must be sexy. It's truly shocking. There will always be stereotypes and I can never change that even though I wish I could, BUT, I can inform you on how diverse both sides can be!

Sexy Concepts are usually thought of as too promiscuous for most people, where they advert their eyes or pretend they have no idea what's going on. It's almost as if women aren't allowed to be sexy in any way, only innocent. Either way, here are some good songs that portray sexy concepts, which should NOT be frowned upon! Sadly there have been girl groups stopped in the international airport overseas in the mind of border protection, believing these girls were coming for prostitution purposes.

Cute Concepts for boys are just as frowned upon for some reason. Many people think cute should stick with girl groups, which I completely disagree with! I think anybody has the right to pull off whatever concept, and cute concepts for boys are fresh and very different from what is usually okay. Here are some songs that fit the cute concept!

One of people's favorite concepts in girl groups and boy groups, the music is amazing in an old-timey way. This concept is kind of slept on because most people never hear anyone talking about it. This is exactly the same as the Girl Group concepts but simply in boy groups.

This is a concept that is scarce with girl groups, usually even around Halloween time there are spooky but cute themed videos, which is okay, but doesn't give you the Halloween feel like some of the boy group songs which is sad, because scary shouldn't equal scandalous if it doesn't with boy groups.

Unlike their female counterparts, Boy groups can freely do as they please when it comes to Halloween. There are bunches more scary themed videos which are detailed and amazing. This isn't a very rare concept for them.

Why do they split and go solo?

People all over the world dream of being pop stars, but perhaps nowhere else more than South Korea, while their northern neighbors are wondering where the next meal is coming from, South Koreans are obsessing over every detail of their K-Pop stars' lives and striving to be as much like them as possible. This regularly leads to really weird and creepy incidents, but those "lucky" enough to actually be an idol are still expected to appreciate it, no matter what hell they're put through. The music might be groovy and the dance moves peppy, but peek under the surface and the K-Pop world is swarming with all kinds of metaphorical maggots.

Most of the groups that have split up have been girl groups, because boy bands may be "better investments. On average, album sales for boy bands majorly surpass girl groups and boys go on way more tours in Asia. In the end, it feels like there is ultimately a shorter investment window with girl groups who do tend to sell more singles than boy bands, but that doesn't help the bottom line as much as album sales and tours would and it seems like those factors would make a group quicker to throw in the towel.

CHAPTER FIVE:
K-POP CHARACTERISTICS

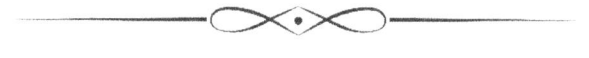

Management agencies in South Korea offer binding contracts to potential artists, sometimes at a young age. Trainees live together in a regulated environment and spend many hours a day learning music, dance, foreign languages, and other skills in preparation for their debut. This "robotic" system of training is often criticized by Western media outlets. In 2012, The Wall Street Journal reported that the cost of training one Korean idol under SM Entertainment averaged US$3 million.

Hybrid genre and transnational values

K-pop is a cultural product that features "values, identity and meanings that go beyond their strictly commercial value." It is characterized by a mixture of modern Western sounds and African-American influences (including sounds from Hip-hop, R&B, Jazz, black pop, soul, funk, techno, disco, and house) with a Korean aspect of performance (including synchronized dance moves, formation changes and the so-called "point choreography" consisting of hooking and repetitive key movements). It has been remarked that there is a "vision of modernization" inherent in Korean pop culture. For some, the transnational values of K-pop are responsible for its success.

A commentator at the University of California, San Diego has said that "contemporary Korean pop culture is built on transnational flows taking place across, beyond, and outside national and institutional boundaries." Some examples of the transnational values inherent in K-pop that may appeal to those from different ethnic, national, and religious backgrounds include a dedication to high-quality output and presentation of idols, as well as their work ethic and polite social demeanor, made possible by the training period.

A woman and a man holding microphones, the men are gesturing to one side. Hip-hop artist Yoon Mi-rae and her husband, rapper Tiger JK of Drunken Tiger, are credited with popularizing American-style hip hop in Korea.

Modern K-pop is marked by its use of English phrases. Jin Dal Yong of Popular Music and Society wrote that the user may be influenced by "Korean-Americans and/or Koreans who studied in the U.S. [who] take full advantage of their English fluency and cultural resources that are not found commonly among those who were raised and educated in Korea." Korean pop music from singers or groups who are Korean-

American such as Fly to the Sky, g.o.d, Rich, Yoo Seung-jun, and Drunken Tiger has both American style and English lyrics.

These Korean-American singers' music has a different style from common Korean music, which attracts the interest of young people. Increasingly, foreign songwriters and producers are employed to work on songs for K-pop idols, such as will.i.am and Sean Garrett. Foreign musicians, including rappers such as Akon, Kanye West, Ludacris, and Snoop Dogg, have also featured on K-pop songs.

The entertainment companies help to expand K-pop to other parts of the world through a number of different methods. Singers need to use English since the companies want to occupy markets in the other parts of Asia, which enables them to open the Western market in the end. Most of the K-pop singers learn English because it is a common language in the world of music, but some singers also learn other foreign languages such as Japanese to approach the Japanese market. Similarly, increasing numbers of K-pop bands use English names rather than Korean ones. This allows songs and artists to be marketed to a wider audience around the world.

However, the use of English has not guaranteed the popularity of K-pop in the North American market. For some commentators, the reason for this is because the genre can be seen as a distilled version of Western music, making it difficult for K-pop to find acceptance in these markets. Furthermore, Western audiences tend to place emphasis on authenticity and individual expression in music, which the idol system can be seen as suppressing.

According to Elaine W. Chun's research, even though hybridity appears more and more often in K-pop, and sometimes may even make fans admire K-pop stars more because it is fresh, new and interesting, it is hard to change those who believe in a perfect ideal for pure linguistic. This means that the original form of language is still difficult to alter.

Artist names, song titles, and lyrics have exhibited significant growth in the usage of English words. No singers in the top fifty charts in 1990 had English in their names: people who worked in the Korean music industry viewed using Korean names as standard. In 1995, most popular singers such as Kim Gun-mo, Park Mi-Kyung, Park Jin-young, Lee Seung-Chul, and Byun Jin-sub still used Korean names, but fourteen of the singers and groups in the top fifty used English names, including DJ DOC, 015B, Piano, and Solid. After the 1997 financial crisis, the government stopped censoring English lyrics and Korea started to have a boom in English. Since the late 1990s, English usage in singers' names, song titles, and lyrics has grown quickly.

Seventeen singers in the top fifty charts used English names in 2000, and thirty-one did so in 2005. In 2010, forty-one singers used English names among the top fifty songs, but usually, three or four singers and groups had more than one or two songs on the chart simultaneously. Korean names (e.g. Baek Ji-young, Seo In-young, and Huh Gak) are seen less frequently, and many K-pop singers have English names (e.g. IU, Sister, T-ara, GD & TOP, Beast, and After School).

Notably, until the early 1990s, musicians with English names would transliterate them into hangul, but now singers would use English names written with the Roman alphabet. In 1995, the percentage of song titles using English in the top 50 charts was 8%. This fluctuated between

30% in 2000, 18% in 2005, and 44% in 2010. An example of a Korean song with a large proportion of English lyrics is Kara's "Jumping," which was released at the same time in both Korea and Japan to much success.

Criticism of hybrid identity

There have been critical responses in South Korea regarding, the identity of the genre, since its ascendance. Some of the notable music critics in the region have criticized K-pop as "a industrial label mainly designed to promote the national brand in the global market from the beginning" and argued that it was "not formed spontaneously as a pop culture but created with the orchestrated plan led by the government with commercial considerations" although in fact "the genre has practically no ties with traditional Korean identity". There's also a perspective that the name of the genre was derived from J-pop.

K-Pop has at times faced criticisms from journalists who perceive the music to be formulaic and unoriginal. Some K-Pop groups have been accused of plagiarizing Western music acts as well as other musical acts. [Unreliable source] In addition, K-Pop has been criticized for its reliance on English phrases, with critics dubbing the use of English in titles "meaningless".

K-Pop groups have been regularly accused of cultural appropriation of cultures such as African-American culture, especially due to the frequent use of cornrows and bandanas in idol groups' on-stage styling. K-Pop groups have also been accused of appropriating Native American and Indian cultures. However, debate exists about whether the borrowing of cultural elements from cultures outside of Korea indeed constitutes cultural appropriation, or if this cultural appropriation is negative at all. Scholar Crystal S. Anderson writes that "[a]ppropriating elements of a culture by taking them out of their original context and using them in a completely different way does not automatically constitute negative cultural appropriation."

Marketing

Many agencies have presented new idol groups to an audience through a "debut showcase", which consists of online marketing and television broadcast promotions as opposed to radio. Groups are given a name and a "concept", along with a marketing hook. These concepts are the type of visual and musical theme that idol groups utilize during their debut or comeback. Concepts can change between debuts and fans often distinguish between boy group concepts and girl group concepts.

Concepts can also be divided between general concepts and theme concepts, such as cute or fantasy. New idol groups will often debut with a concept well known to the market to secure a successful first debut. Sometimes sub-units or sub-groups are formed among existing members. Two example subgroups are Super Junior-K.R.Y., which consists of Super

Junior members Kyuhyun, Ryeowook, and Yesung, and Super Junior-M, which became one of the best-selling K-pop subgroups in China.

Online marketing includes music videos posted to YouTube in order to reach a worldwide audience. Prior to the actual video, the group releases teaser photos and trailers. Promotional cycles of subsequent singles are called comebacks even when the musician or group in question did not go on hiatus.

Choreography

Dance is an integral part of K-pop. When combining multiple singers, the singers often switch their positions while singing and dancing by making prompt movements in synchrony, a strategy called "formation changing". The K-pop choreography often includes the so-called "point dance", referring to a dance made up of hooking and repetitive movements within the choreography that matches the characteristics of the lyrics of the song. Super Junior's "Sorry" and Brown Eyed Girls' "Abracadabra" are examples of songs with notable "point" choreography. To choreograph a dance for a song requires the writers to take the tempo into account. According to Ellen Kim, a Los Angeles dancer, and choreographer, a fan's ability to do the same steps must also be considered: Consequently, K-pop choreographers have to simplify movements.

    The training and preparation necessary for K-pop idols to succeed in the industry and dance successfully are intense. Training centers like Seoul's Def Dance Skool develop the dance skills of youth in order to give them a shot at becoming an idol. Physical training is one of the largest focuses at the school, as much of a student's schedule is based around dance and exercise. The entertainment labels are highly selective, so few make it to fame. Students at the school must dedicate their lives to the mastery of dance in order to prepare for the vigorous routines performed by K-pop groups. This, of course, means that the training must continue if they are signed. Companies house much larger training centers for those who are chosen.

    An interview with K-pop choreographer Rino Nakasone lends insight into the process of creating routines. According to Nakasone, her focus is to make dance routines that are flattering for the dancers but also complementary to the music. Her ideas are submitted to the entertainment company as video recordings done by professional dancers. Nakasone mentions that the company and the K-pop artists themselves have input on a song's choreography. Choreographer May J. Lee gives another perspective, telling that her choreography often starts out as expressing the feeling or the meaning of the lyrics. What starts out as small movements turns into a full dance that is better able to portray the message of the song.

Fashion

The emergence of Seo Taiji and Boys in 1992 paved the way for the development of contemporary K-pop groups. The group revolutionized the Korean music scene by incorporating rap and American hip-hop conventions into their music. This adoption of Western-style extended to the fashions worn by the boy band: the members adopted hip-hop aesthetic. Seo and band-mates' outfits for the promotional cycle of "Nan Arayo" included vibrant street-wear such as oversized T-shirts and sweatshirts, windbreakers, overalls were worn with one strap, overalls were worn with one pant leg rolled up, and American sports team jerseys. Accessories included baseball caps worn backward, bucket hats, and do-rags.

As K-pop "was born of post-Seo trends," many acts that followed Seo Taiji and Boys adopted the same fashion style. Deux and DJ DOC can also be seen wearing on-trend hip-hop fashions such as sagging baggy pants, sportswear, and bandanas in their performances. With Korean popular music transforming into youth-dominated media, manufactured teenage idol groups began debuting in the mid and late '90s, wearing coordinated costumes that reflected the popular fashion trends among youth at the time. Hip-hop fashion considered the most popular style in the late '90s, remained, with idol groups H.O.T. and Sechs Kies wearing the style for their debut songs.

The use of accessories elevated the idol's style from everyday fashion to performance costume, like ski goggles (worn either around the head or neck), headphones are worn around the neck, and oversized gloves worn to accentuate choreography moves were widely used. H.O.T.'s 1996 hit "Candy" exemplifies the level of coordination taken into account for idol's costumes, as each member wore a designated color and accessorized with face paint, fuzzy oversized mittens, visors, bucket hats, and earmuffs, and used stuffed animals, backpacks, and messenger bags as props.

While male idol groups' costumes were constructed with similar color schemes, fabrics, and styles, the outfits were worn by each member still maintained individuality. On the other hand, female idol groups of the '90s wore homogeneous costumes, often styled identically. The costumes for female idols during their early promotions often focused on portraying an innocent, youthful image. S.E.S.'s debut in 1997, "I'm Your

Girl", and Baby Vox's 1998 debut, "Ya Ya Ya", featured the girls dressed in white outfits, "To My Boyfriend" by Fin.K.L shows idols in pink schoolgirl costumes, and "One" and "End" of Chakra presented indu and African style costumes.

To portray a natural and somewhat saccharine image, the accessories were limited to large bows, pompom hair ornaments, and hair bands. With the maturation of female idol groups and the removal of bubblegum pop in the late 1990s, the sets of female idol groups focused on following the fashion trends of the time, many of which were revealing pieces. The latest promotions of the girl groups Baby Vox and Jewelry exemplify these trends of hot pants, micro-miniskirts, crop tops, peasant blouses, transparent garments and blouses on the upper part of the torso.

In the early 1990s and 2000s, ulzzang culture emerged as good looking internet celebrities posted photos on popular sites like Haduri (a face webcam site) and Daum forums. As the rise of ulzzang style paralleled the K-pop phenomenon, many K-pop idols adopted the look, which is described as "huge, delicate Bambi-like eyes with double lids and a tiny, delicate nose with a high bridge ... [s]mooth, pale snow-white skin, and rosebud lips ... a small and sharp chin to achieve the perfect "V-line" face, which should ideally be no bigger than the size of your palm". This look was nearly impossible to gain naturally, giving rise to the popularity of circle contact lenses, plastic surgeries, and skin-whitening products. The industry has been criticized for its narrow beauty standards.

As K-pop became a modern hybrid of Western and Asian cultures starting from the late 2000s, fashion trends within K-pop reflected diversity and distinction as well, fashion trends from the late 2000s to early 2010s can largely be categorized under the following:

Street: focuses on individuality; features bright colors, mix-and-match styling, graphic prints, and sports brands such as Adidas and Reebok.

Retro: aims to bring back "nostalgia" from the 1960s to 1980s; features dot prints and detailed patterns. Common clothing items include denim jackets, boot-cut pants, wide pants, hair bands, scarves, and sunglasses.

Sexy: highlights femininity and masculinity; features revealing outfits made of satin, lace, fur, and leather. Common clothing items include mini-skirts, corsets, net stockings, high heels, sleeveless vests, and see-through shirts.

Black & White emphasizes modern & chic, symbolizes elegance & charisma, mostly applied to formal wear appeal.

Futurism: commonly wore with electronic and hip-hop genres; features popping color items, metallic details, and prints; promotes a futuristic outlook.

K-pop has a significant influence on fashion in Asia, where trends started by idols are followed by young audiences. Some idols have established status as fashion icons, such as G-Dragon and CL, who has repeatedly worked with fashion designer Jeremy Scott, being labeled his "muse".

Government support

The Bank of Korea has attributed the rapid surge in cultural exports since 1997 to the increased worldwide popularity of K-pop.

The South Korean government has acknowledged benefits to the country's export sector as a result of the Korean Wave (it was estimated in 2011 that a US$100 increase in the export of cultural products resulted in a US$412 increase in exports of other consumer goods including food, clothes, cosmetics, and IT products) and thus has subsidized certain endeavors.

Government initiatives to expand the popularity of K-pop are mostly undertaken by the Ministry of Culture, Sports, and Tourism, which is responsible for the worldwide establishment of Korean Cultural Centers. South Korean embassies and consulates have also organized K-pop concerts outside the country, and the Ministry of Foreign Affairs regularly invites overseas K-pop fans to attend the annual K-Pop World Festival in South Korea.

In addition to reaping economic benefits from the popularity of K-pop, the South Korean government has been taking advantage of the influence of K-pop in diplomacy. In an age of mass communication, soft power (pursuing one's goals by persuading stakeholders using cultural and ideological power) is regarded as a more effective and pragmatic diplomatic tactic than the traditional diplomatic strategy hard power (obtaining what one wants from stakeholders through direct intimidation such as military threat and economic sanctions). Cultural diplomacy through K-pop is a form of soft power.

An example of the South Korean government effort in diplomacy through K-pop is the Mnet Asian Music Awards, a K-pop music award ceremony. Park Geun-Hye (the Korean president at the time) delivered the opening statement at the 2014 Mnet Asian Music Awards, which was held in Hong Kong and sponsored by the Korean Small and Medium Business Administration (SMBA). This event was considered a deliberate endeavor by the Korean government to support Korean cultural industries in order to strengthen the nation's international reputation and political influence.

Another example of cultural diplomacy is K-pop performances in North Korea. Prior to 2005, South Korean pop singers occasionally gave performances in North Korea. After an interval of more than a decade, approximately 190 South Korean performers, including well-known musicians Red Velvet, Lee Sun-hee, Cho Yong-Pil, and Yoon Do-Hyun, performed in Pyongyang, North Korea, on March 31 and April 3, 2018. Kim Jong-un was present in the audience.

Copyrights

K-pop music is easy to find online. This is because the Korean entertainment companies holding copyright are not much attached to the copyright regime, but they are willing to share their music through YouTube and other SNS.

CHAPTER SIX:
THE DARK SIDES OF THE KPOP INDUSTRY

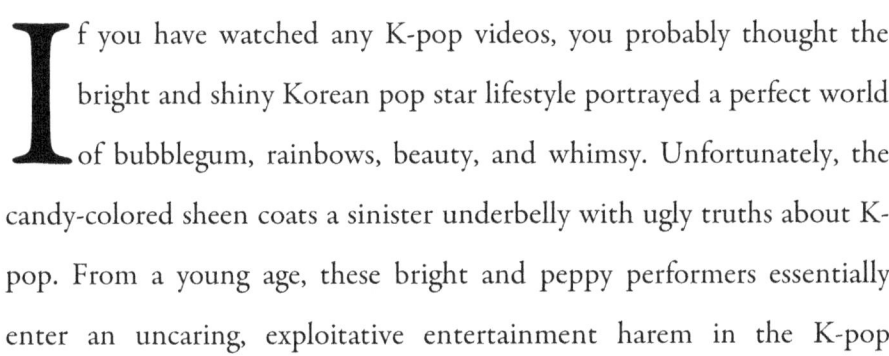

If you have watched any K-pop videos, you probably thought the bright and shiny Korean pop star lifestyle portrayed a perfect world of bubblegum, rainbows, beauty, and whimsy. Unfortunately, the candy-colored sheen coats a sinister underbelly with ugly truths about K-pop. From a young age, these bright and peppy performers essentially enter an uncaring, exploitative entertainment harem in the K-pop industry.

Any faction of the entertainment world is bound to have its secrets; sometimes these are dark yet open secrets overlooked because of convenience or greed. However, what's going on in the K-pop industry isn't hidden: Children who grew up in the industry as manufactured pop products have exposed the mental and physical abuse they suffered through their careers.

From what K-pop trainees endure at the start of their "boot camps" to the suicide attempts, racism, and sexual and physical assaults, the truth about K-pop stars and their industry is anything but glamorous.

Music Executives Have Extreme Control over Stars' Personal Lives

In the year 1940s Hollywood executives were notorious for having a substantial amount of control over their movie stars. Actors were under multiyear and multi-film contracts; they dealt with abuse, stringent rules, and relative ownership at the hands of the studios. Modern K-pop groups experience a similar system, where three major management companies dominate the industry: YG, SM, & JYP.

Members of Korean idol groups have little freedom over their personal lives. As a manufactured entity meant for "selling dreams," they must uphold their employer's image at all times. In many cases, this includes not eating or doing anything too seemingly "independent" in the realm of politics. Consider the case of Taiwanese K-pop idol Chou Tzuyu, who waved a Taiwanese flag during a televised performance, then had to apologize for it publicly.

Many Idols Go Through a 10-Year Pop Star Boot Camp

When a K-pop performer agrees to a contract, it's not only for a record deal; they basically sign their life away to a permanent commitment. An agency trains future stars, many of whom are in adolescence, in a range of performance arts - such as acting, vocals, and dance - for 10 to 15 years before the stars appear in any public act.

Although the agency has a supposed commitment to training their performers in a type of "boot camp," industry leaders often take advantage of their trainees. The agencies make these contracts last for over a decade at times, so if an idol chooses to back out, they need to pay a hefty fee.

These contracts open the door for the agencies to virtually turn the trainees into slaves. Korean laws allow agencies with "touring artists" to work their "employees" as much as they want, even if it means keeping them from sleeping, as in the case of 2 AM idol Jo Kwon.

Idols Are Expected To Get Plastic Surgery

Plastic surgery is far more common in Korea than in the United States. Whereas 1 in 20 women in the US may undergo plastic surgery at some point, the statistics for Korean women claim 1 in 5 chooses to go under the knife.

With plastic surgery being more culturally accepted and often promoted, the standards of beauty have changed, and many teens also desire plastic surgery. Many agencies force idols to undergo surgery - sometimes multiple times - to achieve a "perfect" look and uphold their aspirational aesthetic.

Most stars do not openly discuss their plastic surgery, in part to maintain their idol image, but their physical changes are usually apparent, especially around their eyes, lips, and noses. The average viewer might not notice the differences at first glance, but a plastic surgeon can spot them immediately.

Managers Reportedly Blackmail Their Idols

It's difficult for K-pop singers to break their contracts. In some cases, it's nearly impossible because of the substantial penalties and fines. If a music agency doesn't want to cut ties with an idol yet, they're reportedly not above blackmailing the person to compel them to stay. Managers were even known to film their idols' sexual activities and use the footage against them.

K-pop idol Baek Ji-young's manager filmed her having sex and brought out the footage when she wanted to change contracts. She thought he was bluffing until he put the video on the internet. She tried to sue him, but he fled to the United States, where authorities apprehended him for statutory rape. She claimed her career was nearly ruined by the incident and took years off before returning to the music scene. Fortunately, in 2017 a movement emerged to end the "slave contracts," giving stars more autonomy over their health and well-being.

Music Agencies Allegedly Pimp Their Trainees to Sponsors

In the K-pop industry, music agencies reportedly make demeaning sponsor contracts between idol trainees and sponsors. These celebrity sponsors basically receive an idol to have their way with, mediated only via the contract devised by the idol's employer.

Sponsor contracts allegedly operate under a rigorous ranking system. Depending on the idol involved, the contract's duration and pay rate may vary. It all happens systematically: A potential sponsor reaches out to the idol via a sponsoring broker, and the broker sets up the pay rate per session and terms, which usually includes a period of between six months to one year.

Idols Resort to Starvation to Achieve the 'Perfect' Body Image

As manufactured idols of commercial art, K-pop stars must uphold a particular aesthetic at all times. Being an idol in K-pop requires a look catering to extreme distortions of beauty - specifically, toothpick-thin bodies. While some pop stars adhere to strict diets, others admit they starve themselves.

Sojung of girl group Ladies' Code admits she dieted so much, her hormone levels lowered to "those of a menopausal woman." One-Key from Global Icon allegedly consumed only one bottle of soy milk per day; the rapper reportedly lost nearly 20 pounds in a month. Notably, performer T.O.P purportedly lost almost 50 pounds in a five-week period after restricting his diet to water and the occasional red bean jelly.

Some Idols Follow the Extreme 'Paper Cup Diet'

K-pop idols openly advocate unhealthy dieting. Food-specific regimens, such as the "banana diet" and the "watermelon diet," have become fads in South Korea after idols announced these diets helped them maintain a slender body.

Girl group Nine Muses claimed to find success using the "paper cup diet," which involves consuming nine paper cups' worth of food a day.

The contents of these paper cups weren't specified in their diet - it's simply nine cups of whatever the person chooses to put in them, such as rice, grains, fruit, and anything except refined sugar.

The limited calorie intake for idols and their die-hard fans is alarming. They're consuming insufficient daily calories and starving their bodies to match an unrealistic image of perfection.

Fans Go To Extreme Lengths to Get Close With Stars

In Korean culture, "saying fans" are the rabid devotees of the K-pop industry. They know no boundaries or rules when it comes to their idol obsession, often engaging in stalking or other irrational behaviors.

Because of toxic idolization, a fan's devotion sometimes can lead to obscene acts and invasions of privacy.

One K-pop manager revealed his personal experience with these fans, exposing the horrors of obsession. He says the taxi-following fans are actually the docile ones - things can get much worse for people who take their stunning to extremes. Not only have sasaeng fans broken into his building multiple times, they once spread urine and feces all over his doorstep, as if to mark their territory.

Managers and Executives Take Advantage of Rising Stars

Jang Suk-woo, Open World Entertainment's CEO and talent coach, was a notorious sex offender to the aspiring idols who walked through his doors. As the executive in charge of screening talent and coaching young celebrities, he took advantage of his position. He allegedly drugged and sexually assaulted his trainees from November 2010 - March 2012.

Eventually, authorities disbanded his harem of young idols. Charged under the Children and Youth Protection Act, his sentence entailed six years of jail time. In 2017 the CEO of another K-pop agency was "brokering his agency's female trainees." His penalty included a fine and prison sentence.

Idols Regularly Faint Onstage

K-pop idols routinely starve themselves and push their bodies to unhealthy physical limitations. Because of this, it's not uncommon for an idol to collapse during a performance.

Without sleep or proper nutrients, the human body can function for only so long. Fainting is a fairly frequent occurrence for these overworked celebrities. The K-pop industry's competitive nature doesn't allow much slack, but these idols are not robots. Though the music industry is competitive, this doesn't undermine the artists' need for self-care.

Idols Often Take Years to Make Money

K-pop is a massive, multibillion-dollar industry raking in cash, thanks to everything from merchandise sales to stadium tickets. Regardless, K-pop stars see little to none of this fortune. Idols' contracts are often so restrictive; some have likened them to slavery. While idols sing, dance, and push themselves to the point of starvation, the celebrities driving this massive market are victims of financial exploitation.

In an explosive video on January 2018, former K-pop star Prince Mak claimed K-pop's "break-even" system, created by the studios, ensures idols repay the amount invested in them during their training. These costs include accommodations, staff, food, and music video production.

According to Mak, an average K-pop group earns about $4,000 per show, 90% of which goes directly to the company. Once the group members split the remaining 10%, they put it toward their debts to the studio. Mak used the group AOA as an example - though they started touring in 2012, they didn't turn a profit until 2015.

Industry executives insist K-pop is expensive to produce and manufacture, arguing it's highly competitive and financially demanding. With CDs becoming obsolete and digital music sales bringing far less revenue than before, the residuals performing members receive barely reflect their hard work.

Anti-Fans Sometimes Try To Kill Idols

K-pop idols have some serious haters. These "anti-fans" create such extreme competition in their mind; they may attempt to kill despised idols. One chilling incident involved an anti-fan and Yunho, a member of the K-pop duo TVXQ.

During a public event, the idol accepted a presumed orange-juice-based cocktail, but he later recalled, "Suddenly, I ended up coughing up blood, and I vomited and passed out." Yunho spent several days in the hospital - the drink turned out to contain a potentially deadly mixture of orange juice and superglue.

After recovering, Yunho heard from the anti-fan: "I was angry at first, but the anti-fan told me that he hated seeing me laugh on TV when he was going through hard times, so I realized that I could be a harmful influence on other people."

Among other troubling incidents surrounding K-pop stars and anti-fans is the Jay Park petition, a list of signatures calling for the idol's suicide after he announced his departure from popular group 2 PM.

Racism & Cultural Insensitivity Abound In The Idol Industry

Idol industry executives reportedly prefer talent whose ethnicity is 100% Korean and often on the fairer-skinned side. Though younger generations of Koreans show more progressive and open-minded views, racism is still rampant in Korea, particularly toward darker-skinned people.

Idols are sometimes extraordinarily discriminatory and culturally insensitive to other ethnicities. K-pop girl group Mamamoo faced backlash after releasing a video for their cover of Bruno Mars's "Uptown Funk," during which they wore offensive blackface makeup. Though the group later apologized and said they didn't realize the implications of their actions, this was not the first time blatant bigotry appeared in K-pop.

Being LGBTQ+ Is Considered Taboo, Although a Few Stars Have Come Out

The first openly LGBTQ+ K-pop idol, Holland, made his debut in January 2018. However, being queer publicly is taboo both in South Korea and the K-pop industry, which leads to speculative rumors and trauma for those who identify as LGBTQ+.

According to one underground thread, a female K-pop idol outed herself as a lesbian during an interview. Although the news reportedly spread through the industry, her music agency deleted the footage and made a serious attempt to keep everything quiet. Allegedly, the agency coerced the star to undergo a "conversion therapy" process, after which she attempted suicide.

The story was not officially confirmed, however, and agencies often try to cover up conversations involving the LGBTQ+ community as it relates to K-pop. Music is a commercial industry - deviating from the norm can have consequences.

A Misogynistic Double Standard Exists When It Comes To Male & Female Idols

According to industry insiders, up-and-coming female K-pop stars experience intense harassment from male idols; one writer called the world of K-pop "a misogynistic playground." Etiquette requirements skew strongly in favor of male pop stars, and the male-dominated executive rank at management companies and studios perpetuates a toxic environment.

There are abundant written exposés about the "gross double standard" in K-pop. One writer cited how some women in K-pop develop a forced submission to authority and face stigmatization from slander, while men's reputations can survive scandals more easily in comparison.

Idols Aren't Allowed to Date Other Stars

According to Quartz, "K-pop stars are expected to be near-perfect role models for their fans. Often this means a public love life is out of the question." Stoking fan fantasy is part of the end goal of stringent management, which means cultivating the appearance of attractive, datable (single) stars for the audience.

In 2014 dating rumors leaked about an idol from boy band EXO and a member of Girls' Generation. The two apologized to their fans, publicly stating their sorrow for how they "hurt" them. Japanese pop idol Minami Minegishi, from the girl band AKB48, shaved her head and made a tearful public apology after breaking a clause in her contract forbidding her from spending the night with her boyfriend.

South Korea is reportedly more lenient than Japan and Taiwan when it comes to rules regarding pop stars dating, but the perception remains crucial. Ultimately, the business side of the industry treats K-pop as a product, not an art form, so interests lie in maintaining investments.

Music Agencies Foster Intense Rivalries between Girl Groups

Rumor has it, music agencies contrive intense rivalries between K-pop girl groups. Managers reportedly cut off communication between the groups when they make public appearances, telling them not to talk to girls who are beneath them. Though they seem put-together and bubblegum-friendly on the surface, it's only a smokescreen to perpetuate their idol status to the audience.

The girls might be friendly to each other on camera, but it's not hard to imagine the effects of long hours, manager-driven tension, and starvation diets on backstage relationships.

Struggling With Mental Health Is Stigmatized

After Shinee member Jong-hyun's suicide in 2017, a conversation sparked around mental health and the well-being of K-pop stars and other Korean entertainers. Idols often work grueling hours on little food and sleep, plus endure duress from the public. Even so this is one of few that has gone very wrong, recently in 2019 former Kara member Hara explained her self as she was on the breach of suicide: "I'm truly sorry for causing concern due to the recent event. I am currently recovering my health."

"I was feeling distressed due to various incidents that piled up. I will try my best to show a healthy side of myself by having a stronger mindset. I am truly sorry about the recent incident."

Slave Contracts Are Normal

When a contract you sign is colloquially called a "slave contract," you might want to think twice. One of the major problems with K-Pop contracts is that stars basically sign their lives away. According to the pop star Prince Mak, you might sign a contract that pays for the next seven to 15 years you have to stay with the group and do exactly what you are told. Maybe that doesn't sound so bad; after all, it's less than what you'd get for murder, right? And this contract comes with the perks of being famous.

Except not really, the catch is that the contract years only start "counting down" once you have your "debut" as a star, and that could take a while, you might be trained for up to ten years before you ever set foot on a stage or in a recording studio.

Even once you become a household name, things don't get better because that long-term contract you signed probably didn't leave room for you to make any money. No matter how famous you get, slavery doesn't pay. When members of girl band Stellar told No Cut News about their rise to fame, the four girls said they regularly split one meal because they were so broke. In one bright spot, the BBC reported that boy band Dong

Bang Shin Ki won a court case over a 13-year, low-pay contract. But they're one of the biggest K-Pop bands of all time, so don't the rest of you get your hopes up.

Like other areas of entertainment, K-Pop has a casting couch. Because of your slim chances of success and how much power management has, you might find yourself at any moment bartering sex for fame. In K-Pop it might be called "sponsorship" or "transactions," but at the end of the day, it's selling your body for success. Seoul Beats said one girl was even asked to marry a powerful guy she had no interest in.

Being a K-Pop star can also be an in-road to an acting career. In 2010, Korea Joongang Daily reported that 60 percent of actresses were expected to sexually pay for roles in some way. Actresses have even been known to kill themselves over the expectation of prostitution.

Even if you haven't ever sold sex for favors in your life, that doesn't mean you're safe from suspicion. According to LA Weekly, the eight-member girl band Oh My Girl was held for 15 hours at LAX after customs officials mistook them for prostitutes in 2015. Part of the problem was they referred to themselves as "sisters" (a normal term of endearment in Korea) when it was clear they were not blood-related and they had a lot of sexy clothes in their suitcases. This sent up red flags to the officers and it took a while until the problem was sorted out. Young, hot Asian chicks, beware: There's obviously no reason you'd be coming to America except to sell your bodies.

The hours are nuts

You'd think that the work hours of a pop star are better than, say, those of a lawyer. Isn't it part of the whole "being famous" package that, yeah, you have to work nights but at least you get to sleep in? Maybe in some countries but not when you sign your soul over to become a K-Pop star. Say goodbye to sleep for the next decade.

According to Seoul Beats, you can forget money or fancy cars because sleep is a pop star's greatest luxury. SBS Pop Asia says that an average workday can be 20 hours, leaving just a few hours for sleep. That might be possible to pull off once or twice in a row, but this is all day every day. And in between those precious few hours, you constantly have a camera in your face, so you better be peppy and look gorgeous. That's probably why being hospitalized for exhaustion is just par for the course when you're a K-Pop star. Krystal, of f(x), has fainted on a screen so many times it's almost become a kind of trademark. At one point she was doing a gig and passed out with the mic still in her hand because that is professionalism.

KpopStarz reports that one over-worked individual, SHINee's Minho, finally got some time off and fell asleep at a friend's house - for 48 hours. Yeah, he was so tired he didn't wake up for two days, and it wasn't even in his own bed.

CHAPTER SEVEN:
THE DIFFICULT LIFE OF A KPOP IDOL

Why Life In The Business Is Hard

For over one decade, Korean pop has been overtaking the world. Whether you are a fan of Korean pop or not, you will admit that at least one Korean pop song rings in your head for days after the first time you hear it. Distinct for their synchronized dance moves and catchy music, the kpop music industry is often likened to a factory that churns out idol groups in high numbers every year.

Thanks to the global success of top-rated artists such as EXO, Girls Generation, and Big Bang, the vast majority of teenagers look up to them and dream of becoming like them. In a bid to try their luck, multitudes of the teenagers go on to audition at leading entertainment agencies such as SM Entertainment, YG Entertainment, JYP Entertainment, and many more. However, truth be told, being a Kpop idol isn't just having a fantastic talent and good looks to complement it. Being a kpop star, a successful one at that takes skill, good looks, tears, sweat, and blood.

Now, for those people who enjoy listening to Korean pop music these days and are fans of kpop idols, the majority have no idea of the hard work and difficulties their idols had to go through or had gone through.

To become a kpop idol, first, you need to sign up at a company and then train to become an idol. There are a number of companies nowadays that help to train idols, and the bigger the company is, the harder it is for the prospective idol to getting into. Though some companies hold auditions for newcomers, who want to become kpop idols. While several auditions are held every year, it's quite tricky for a newcomer to excel at the auditions since several people are at the auditions.

For instance, you go for an audition, when you excel at the auditions, and you enter into a contract with the company, you get the "Trainee" title. When TMJ became a trainee, the next thing to do is to sign up for dancing, singing, acting lessons, and language classes. Truth be told, life as a Trainee is hard, no thanks to the tight schedules. Some trainees who still go to college will have to attend the training classes after school, and that will be hard since they have to go to school first and then the lessons after.

For trainees, the training hours last for four hours or more, starting from 6pm thereabout to 10pm. For trainees in JYP company, they have to undergo one to five classes daily, with each class lasting for 3 hours. Now you can see that becoming a kpop idol isn't a day job. Heck, a trainee can spend 5 hours or more every day practicing dancing, especially when the monthly evaluations are coming. Yeah, there are monthly evaluations. The trainee needs to train hard for the review so he or she can show the company the progress made else they are thrown out of the program.

In addition to the rigorous daily training, trainees are also given daily homework to do, and in the instance where the homework isn't done, they are left behind by the company. So many trainees who had high hopes of becoming a kpop idol give up on their dreams thanks to the tight schedules and rigorous pieces of training they go through in order not to get thrown out of the company.

The tight schedule isn't the only reason why life in the business is hard. No, it isn't the only hurdle a trainee has to cross, there's also the issue of weight management. Some trainees who are big on the weight side will have to lose weight while others may have to maintain their current weight, which is difficult because of the daily training and exercises. They also have to watch what they eat to keep their weight in check. This means that they may need to stay away from certain foods though it also depends on the rules of the company. Some companies go as far as checking the weight of the trainees daily to see if they have their weight in check in to be.

After training a while, there's a chance a trainee will go on to debut, but not all trainees make the cut. To debut, a trainee must have been training for a while, with the average training period being 2-4 years though the training period varies for each trainee. For instance, Jo Kwon, a member of the balled group 2am was a trainee for about 7 years before debuting while Kyuhyun, a member of the Super Junior group, trained only for 3 months before debuting.

The life of a trainee is hard and so tiring that many trainees give up on their dreams before they get to the finish line. But for the trainees that persevere till the finish line, they get accepted into the company, and they sign a contract. The only downside is leaving the company is quite difficult. A trainee who chooses to leave the training period before his or her contract with the company has ended will have to pay the company back the time and effort the company puts into training them.

While so many people out there who listen to Korean pop wish to train to become a kpop idol themselves, becoming one is quite hard.

To become a kpop idol, you have to start at the trainee level, where you will undergo rigorous training. The training period can be years, and there is a chance that you may or may not debut. The life of a kpop trainee will be a little easy if only companies can give them alone time to enjoy themselves. Trainees need time to rest so their bodies can regain the energies that have been lost from training. Many kpop idols and trainees have landed in the hospitals because they overworked their bodies and didn't get enough sleep. More importantly, companies should let them eat healthy instead of eating less.

As there are many bad sides found in all types of industries all over the world, we just need to be aware of what these people go through to become an idol. In the end, the results are stunning and entertaining in all its aspect.

Thanks for reading this book. I hope you'll take your time to leave an honest review for the next reader to pick up this book, thanks again!

Made in the USA
Coppell, TX
19 March 2020